know
the
game

Float Fishing

by Colin Dyson
Co-editor of COARSE ANGLER
magazine

Published by A & C Black (Publishers) Ltd
35 Bedford Row, London WC1R 4JH

Contents

Introduction

Many people who do not fish wonder why they seldom see anglers catching anything. One answer is that they mostly observe anglers in crowded public places where they stand little chance anyway. Another prime cause of failure is that many anglers fish with the wrong floats in the wrong places. It has been estimated, almost certainly correctly, that only ten per cent of all anglers perform efficiently for most of the time. Nobody learns the subtle arts of float fishing in a short time, but to have an approach which is basically correct is as easy as being wrong. The purpose of this book is to help angling beginners of all ages to be right more often than they are wrong. I shall try to write the book which was not there to help me when I started. I blundered along for years, learning slowly by myself, but the pace speeded up considerably when I stopped being a journalistic all-rounder and began to specialise in angling.

It has been my privilege to fish with some of the finest anglers in Britain, and many are now my friends. Much of what I know is due to them, and where special credit is due I will mention it in the text. If I forget a few names I must beg forgiveness in advance, for there have been so many. This book is testimony to my belief that it is possible to learn a great deal by reading and studying diagrams of shotting patterns. But it is also a considerable help to go and watch the experts, whenever the opportunity arises. Regardless of what the specimen-hunting fraternity may say, a big open contest can be very much like an open-air university for an open-minded observer who is keen to learn. All the basic skills are on display, and basic skills catch fish.

There are some who doubt that float fishing is the best way to catch good fish. Legering — a method of fishing without a float and which rates a separate book — is said to produce the whoppers. I used to believe that myself, until I actually sat down and worked out how I had caught my best fish. Legering has accounted for my biggest barbel, but roach to 2 lb, perch to 3 lb 7 oz, rudd to 3 lb 8 oz, chub to 4 lb 15 oz and pike to 25 lb have all been taken on the float. In most of these cases the float had been used in a simple way which anyone can learn.

Float fishing is not as complicated as it might seem to the beginner when he pushes open that tackle shop door for the very first time. The place simply bristles with floats. They hang from the ceiling, sprout from containers on the counter, sparkle invitingly from under glass — manufacturers certainly know how to pander to the magpie instinct, which is present in us all. It would be interesting to know the percentage of floats which are bought solely for their beauty! Hopefully, when you have read this book, you will be a little more discriminating.

The appearance of a float is secondary to how it performs. The colour of the tip, no matter how attractive it appears in the shop, is wrong if you cannot see it properly. Black or white are sometimes the only colours which can be seen against certain backgrounds, especially at a distance, yet black is seldom seen in the shops and white is never used as a tip colour. Orange, yellow and red look nice, but they can only be seen clearly against the kind of dark background that is found on tree-lined water, or where there is some other feature to darken the normally white reflection of the sky. You may think this a trifling point, but it is one of the most important. If a float does everything you want it to do, but you cannot actually see it properly, you are sunk.

But what are the main functions of a float? One obvious function is that it is a bite detection device and it does this in three ways. It can be taken under by a fish, it can be lifted up by a fish which lifts the bottom shot, and it can be held up by a fish intercepting a falling bait. So it is essential to register in your mind the correct setting of the float when it is carrying its normal shotting load. If you know how it should 'sit' on the surface without interference from fish you will be able to recognise the lift and hold up bites, which are not quite so easy as the straightforward runaway!

Another key function of a float is that it helps to deliver the bait to the required depth and distance. The depth setting is easy enough, in most cases, but distance demands the use of a given weight, and the chosen float must carry that weight.

The need to defeat the problem of distance is one of the reasons why there is such a bewildering size range and, to some extent, why so many different materials are used in the construction of floats. The more buoyant the material the more weight it carries and so a greater distance can be achieved.

Finally, another important requirement of a float is that its design assists, or at the very least does not hinder, the correct presentation of a bait. I hope that this does not sound complicated — it can be summed up quite easily: the function of a float is to deliver a bait to the correct distance and depth, and to signal bites. The vast range of circumstances in which floats are used to achieve these aims helps to explain why there are so many shapes and sizes of float.

An example of some of the common floats currently in use.

Hints

Here is some information which should help you to understand the float diagrams and accompanying text.

SHOTS

With rare exceptions, which are beyond the scope of this book, floats are weighted with round split shot of varying sizes. It is simply pinched on the line in the required place. To keep the diagrams simple the full-size range of shot which is available is not shown; also I am quite sure that most anglers do not need the full range. The selection which is used subdivides almost exactly into fractions. The largest size of shot is the **swan**, the next size being the **AAA** (approximately half a swan). A **BB** is half an AAA, a **No. 4** is half a BB, and a **No. 6** is half a No. 4. The only other size I use is the **No. 8**. These are the only shots which will be mentioned in the text and on the diagrams (see Fig. 1).

SWAN   4

AAA   6

BB   8

Fig. 1

FLOAT RUBBERS

These are usually rubber or silicone tubings of varying diameters, and are used to attach some floats to the line. In every case where rubbers are used the float is attached at both the top and the bottom or 'double rubber'.

LOCKING A FLOAT

This is a method sometimes used to attach a float to the line by one end only. The line goes through a ring at the base of the float, and shots are pinched on the line at each side of the ring (see Fig. 2). An alternative favoured by some is to pass the line through the bottom ring several times, laying each turn of line beside the next. The turns have to be loosened to adjust the setting of the float and then re-tightened. Locked shot is the most popular method these days, and floats fished this way are usually called 'wagglers'.

Fig. 2

SINKING THE LINE

So that some floats may be fished efficiently the line has to be sunk to remove it from the influence of the wind or current. Generally, the floats involved are the wagglers. The way to sink the line is to cast beyond the intended spot, and then plunge the rod tip under the water and reel back sharply. Another way is to chop the line under with sharp movements of the rod, parallel to the water. The line will sink more easily if it is wiped with a cloth that has been soaked in detergent.

KNOTS

Although the attachment of hooks to line, and hook lengths to main reel line, is not exactly within the scope of this book it is certainly essential knowledge for those who are trying to

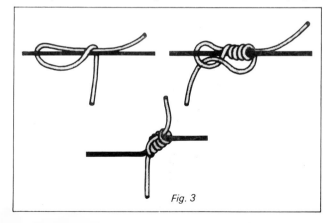

Fig. 3

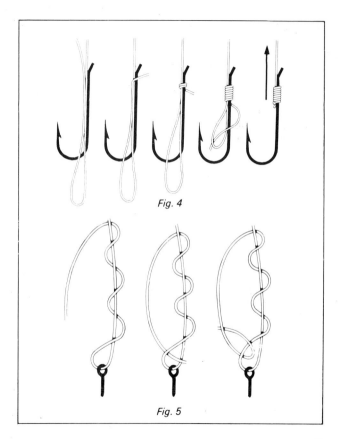

Fig. 4

Fig. 5

5

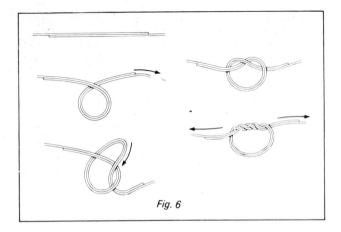

Fig. 6

PLUMBING THE DEPTH

Many fish are caught on or just off the bottom, so it is important for the angler to know exactly how deep the water is. Another advantage of careful plumbing is that it reveals the presence of underwater features, such as a ledge or a depression, which can attract and hold fish.

So, how do you plumb the depth? Nowadays it is possible to buy plummets which clip on to the hook. They are heavy enough to sink the float, so if you drop in at the rod end and the float disappears it is set too shallow; if it stays up top it is too deep. Keep plumbing and adjusting until the tip of the float shows. You then have the exact depth at the rod end. Further plumbing beyond the rod end and along the swim, in the case of a river, will give you a mental picture of the nature of the bottom.

At long range on stillwater the job becomes more time-consuming, and at range on a river it is tricky. In such a case I tend not to use a plummet; I divide the shot that the float carries into two, placing one half under the float and the other on the hook. If the float will not run through without dragging under I know that it is over-depth, and make adjustments until it does stay up. If I start too shallow I keep on deepening until the hook and lead hit the bottom. Naturally, the picture gets complicated if there are bumps in the bottom, but the where-abouts of these are revealed if the tackle always pulls under in the same places. Once the exact depth of the swim is discovered it can pay to pinch a small marker shot on the line. It should be left there no matter how many adjustments are subsequently made to the tackle, so that you can always see how much over or under the depth you are fishing.

translate the words and diagrams into successful angling. Hooking fish is not much use, if they are lost in the next instant! One knot that should be mentioned here is the slider stop knot (see Fig. 3); this knot is used to stop a sliding float at the required depth. Take note of how it is tied. The other illustrations show the spade end knot (Fig. 4), which is used, as you might expect, for tying spade end hooks, and the half blood knot (Fig. 5), which is used for tying eyed hooks. Eyed hooks can be tied direct to the reel line. Spades — and eyed hooks when a hook length of a weaker breaking strain to the reel line is required — are tied to separate lengths of line. It is a simple job to attach these hook lengths to the reel line. There are many knots to choose from, but the water knot is the one I find the most effective (see Fig. 6).

The Floats

The most effective fishing in terms of seeing the bites and striking them successfully is done at close range, where floats can be kept small and very sensitive. Among the most effective for the job are purpose-made canal floats, very small peacock quill floats and the floats used by the roach pole specialists, whose requirements are not really within the scope of this book.

CROWQUILL

With the rod and reel I nearly always use the little peacocks and, sometimes, the forefather of all the close-range floats,

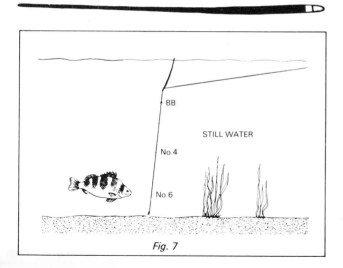

the crowquill, which also has the advantage of being the cheapest to obtain. In my opinion it was purely the swing to fancy floats that saw the crowquill go out of favour and I do not think that any of the newer floats perform better. The diagrams for the crowquill are virtually self-explanatory (see Figs. 7 and 8). It can be used thick or thin side up, double rubber, or thin side up attached bottom only with a tight rubber — the latter method is particularly useful on stillwaters where the wind is awkward. The crowquill is mainly a stillwater float, though it can also be effective at close range on slow-flowing rivers, when it has to be fished double rubber.

BB

STILL WATER

No. 4

No. 6

Fig. 7

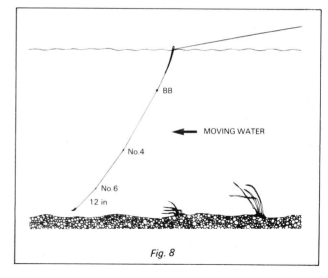

BB

MOVING WATER

No. 4

No. 6

12 in

Fig. 8

CANAL ANTENNA

The Canal Antenna was, I believe, designed by World Champion Billy Lane as an alternative to the crowquill. Apart from commercial considerations he recognised that we cannot all run around yanking tail feathers out of crows, or find suitable feathers which have been shed more naturally! The antenna

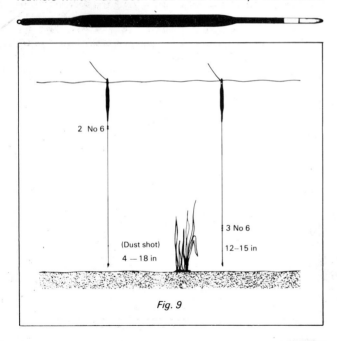

2 No 6

(Dust shot)
4 — 18 in

3 No 6

12–15 in

Fig. 9

has a slim balsa-wood body and an even slimmer insert in the tip, which is made out of cane; it is easily pulled under. The float is always used at short range on a canal or lake, but hardly ever on a river as it is not buoyant enough for moving water.

One shotting pattern is exactly like the crowquill. The main alternatives are to bunch all the shot about 12 in to 15 in from the hook (a dodge which is useful when small fish feeding high in the water are a nuisance, preventing the bait sinking quickly to bigger fish on or near the bottom) or to have a dust shot down the line with the rest of the shot tight under the float (see Fig. 9). This method succeeds when you actually want to catch fish as the bait is slowly falling, and it also works well when the tackle is fished over-depth with the bait hard on the bottom. Mostly, with this float (and the crowquill too, for that matter) the bait is fished just fractionally off the bottom.

LIGHT PEACOCK QUILL

This is another float which does much the same job as the crowquill and the canal antenna, but the peacock is always fished attached bottom only. Also, if the wind is skittish, the peacock is more effective than the crowquill and canal antenna. It is slightly more stable, but once the hook is under the surface the bait is fished in exactly the same way — usually just on or off the bottom — and shotted to sink fast or slow, as required. A fairly standard shotting pattern is illustrated here (see Fig. 10), with a BB and a No. 4 locking the float, a No. 6 around half depth and a No. 6 nearest the hook. This shotting pattern is a favourite of England International, Kevin Ashurst, and his knowledge has influenced the way I fish most of my peacock floats.

Although the light peacock is mostly effective at a range of one to three rod lengths it can be regarded as the most efficient of the peacock range. Greater distance demands bigger floats with different and less sensitive shotting patterns.

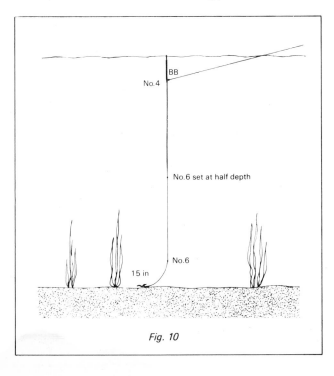

Fig. 10

MEDIUM AND LARGE PEACOCKS

Stillwaters

These are among the most versatile of floats. One golden rule with peacocks is always to choose one which can be cast easily to the required distance. Err on the heavy side, or too many casts will drop short. Peacock quill is an ideal material for making floats because it comes in so many different thicknesses and it is very buoyant. Differing thicknesses enable the enthusiastic home producer to make a wide range of floats for particular purposes and, as it is an easy material to work with,

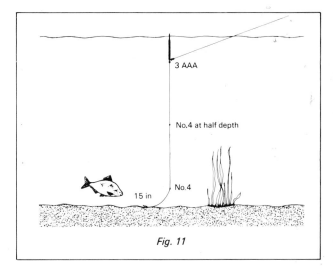

Fig. 11

it does not require too much skill to achieve a float carrying exactly the right amount of shot. I cannot lay down any hard and fast guidelines on size simply because of the differing thicknesses of the quills, which are readily available from good tackle shops. I grade my quills into three bundles — thin (for little floats and for use as inserts in the tips of bigger floats), medium (for most medium and long-range work) and thick (for extreme distances and specialist purposes). Tip inserts, incidentally, are used to make some floats more sensitive.

The aim with peacock quills is to make, or buy a complete range, scaling up from the little 2BB to a maximum of 3 swan shot. Obviously the floats have to get thicker and/or longer as the shot carrying capacity increases. If the original straight shape was maintained, it would eventually wind up with dimensions which were too awkward and unacceptable. The middle and top floats in the peacock family, therefore, have cork or balsa bodies at the base. The sole reason for these bodies is to add shot carrying capacity without unduly changing the length and thickness.

There are many ways to fish the peacock wagglers and several are illustrated here. Fig. 11 is not much more than an enlargement of the close-range peacock described earlier, but there is more to it than is at first apparent. The 3 AAAs locking the float ensure longer casting but note the No. 4s. They are placed in the same positions as the lighter No. 6s in the previous diagram, but as the No. 4s are bigger there is a more marked effect on the tip of the float when a fish either lifts or stops the fall of the bottom shot. It is necessary to emphasise these bites if they are to be readily spotted at long range.

A float carrying about the same amount of shot can be used for a quite different purpose. Fig. 12 shows a much shorter

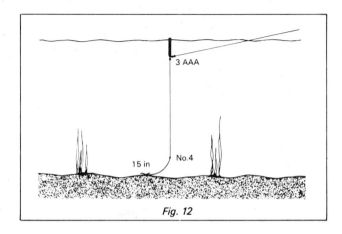

Fig. 12

and fatter peacock taking 3AAAs locking and just a No. 4 down; there is no insert in the tip. When Kevin Ashurst first showed me this one I could not see what it was for. In fact it is used for long casting into shallow water. Long floats in shallow water tend to scare the fish; this one is less obvious to them. Do not expect to see any lift bites with a tip this thick. Fish in shallow water usually pick up a bait and bolt, causing the familiar 'go under' bite.

There are many different ways to shot up for deeper water at medium and long range, but which one to choose often depends upon the way the fish are biting and where they are in the water. A typical pattern (Fig. 13) achieves a longish cast and presents a bait falling at a nice even pace through the water. If the bites are coming early, before the hook has reached

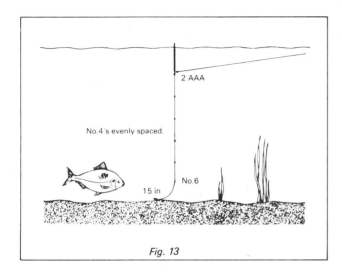

2 AAA

No.4's evenly spaced.

No.6

15 in

Fig. 13

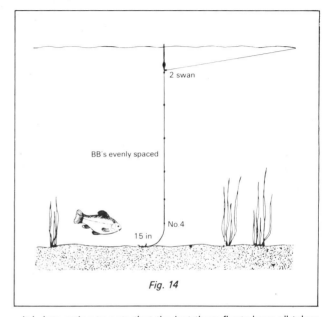

2 swan

BB's evenly spaced

No 4

15 in

Fig. 14

maximum depth, it can pay to stick with this even string of No. 4s and a No. 6 and shorten the depth. You might as well keep the bait at the level inhabited by the fish, instead of having the bait go to and then past them. If, on the other hand, all the bites are coming at a later stage — when the hook has fully sunk — there is a case for a change. The need, here, is to get the hook to sink to the fish more quickly. Why waste time? Slide one, two or even all the No. 4s down to join the one immediately above the No. 6. There is no need to illustrate this bunch and dropper method, as it is called; you can see what is required by mentally amending Fig. 13.

It is interesting to note that the last three floats have all taken approximately the same amount of shot, even if the use has been different and, in the case of Fig. 12, the shape is also different. These three floats are mainly for use on stillwater. Before rivers are discussed, I will illustrate the shotting of a much larger float; this time with a body, for really long-range work in deeper water (Fig. 14). It is merely a scaled up version of Fig. 13, and the shotting can be adjusted in the same manner.

Rivers

Basically there is little difference in the way peacocks are used on rivers. Certainly there is no obvious difference which can be gleaned from mere appraisal of the diagrams. Shotting patterns are practically interchangeable in some cases, but on rivers the wagglers are by no means as easy to control. So the emphasis must switch to the question of control and how the shotting must sometimes be varied to achieve control.

Problems mount as the speed of water increases, so we will start with a simple arrangement for catching roach and small bream from a slow moving river or fenland drain. As you can see from the diagram (Fig. 15) it is very similar to the ones

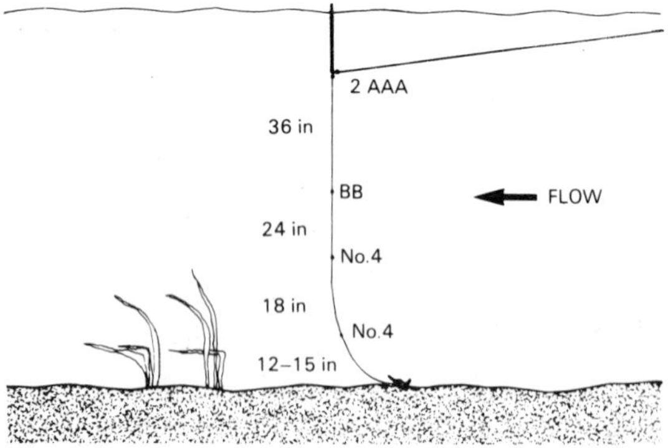

Fig. 15

showing the stillwater rigs. There is just some extra weight, the BB, at half depth to boost the initial sinking speed. River fish are generally on or near the bottom — the better ones that I try to catch, anyway! Watch, as the float settles, for the weight of the BB to register the fact that it has sunk as far as it can go, and then watch for the No. 4s to do the same. A couple of casts should tell you how long it takes. If it seems to be taking longer — strike. This rig will trundle slowly down with the flow with maybe just the hook dragging bottom. If a wind is going in the same direction as the flow it can cause the float to go through too fast. One way to cure this is to deepen the setting of the float to allow the bottom No. 4 to drag. Slowing down a float in this manner can make all the difference between catching and not catching, but it might not always work with the simple adjustment just described. The No. 4 might be too heavy a shot to drag; it could cause the float to pull under. Sometimes a switch to a lighter No. 6 will do the trick; at other times it may be necessary to remove the last but one shot altogether. This would cause more float to stick out of the water, making it more difficult to drag the float under. In theory this offers more resistance to a biting fish, but it does not seem to make much difference to the results.

Perhaps it will help to make the point if I choose another roach rig, slightly heavier this time, and illustrate how it might be fished over even and uneven bottoms. Can you spot the difference between Figs. 16a and 16b? In Fig. 16a the last two shots are a No. 4 dragging, with a BB above, and there is not much sticking out above the surface. Over the uneven bottom in Fig.16b, it is different. The No. 4 has been changed to a No. 6, with a No. 4 above instead of a BB and there is much more of the float sticking above the surface.

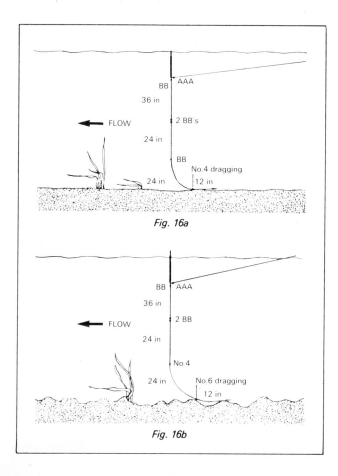

Fig. 16a

Fig. 16b

When a river is moving quickly there is no case for an insert in the tip. It will pull under too easily if the bottom shot and/or the hook is dragging. A thicker tip resists much better, though it will still go under in response to a bite. What usually happens with all of the peacock wagglers used on rivers is that the fish stops the bait and the current pushes the float under almost simultaneously. The heaviest float used on a river would be a 3 swan, shotted as in Fig. 17; this arrangement would be used

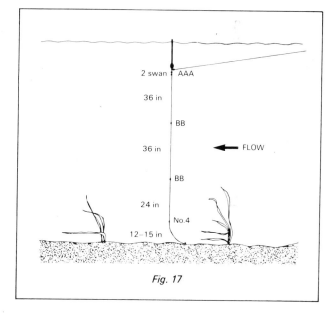

Fig. 17

for distance casting into water around 10 ft deep.

Generally speaking all the peacock wagglers used on rivers are chosen when conditions defeat the use of the double rubber floats. However, there is a degree of overlap. Wagglers are usually fished with the line sunk to defeat nasty winds blowing downstream or into the face. Double rubber floats have shorter ranges, and winds blowing strongly in any direction except upstream, upstream and out, or from straight behind make it difficult to use them effectively. There is one instance in which a double rubber could be used, but which really calls for a small waggler — shallow and fairly fast water, especially if it is clear. Double rubber floats tend to splash on the strike, even in expert hands, and this can scare the fish, whereas wagglers slip under much more silently on the strike and are less frightening for the fish. Fig. 18 shows an excellent rig for this sort of fishing.

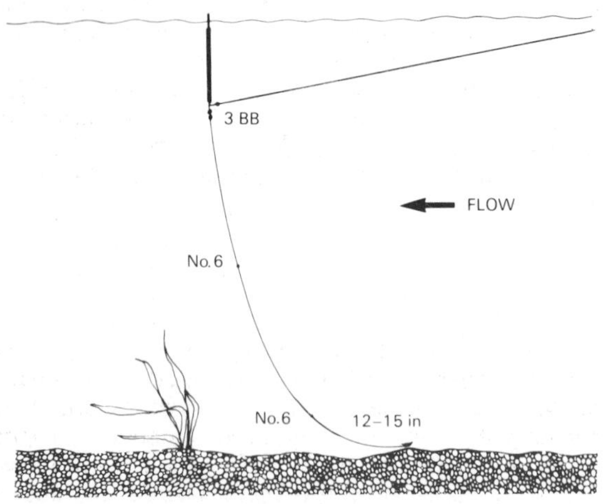

Fig. 18

DOUBLE RUBBER FLOATS

With the exception of extreme close range in ideal conditions, double rubber floats are not used much on stillwaters. Almost without exception they are best used on flowing water of medium to fast pace and at close to medium range; although it should be pointed out that some types can be used efficiently at quite a distance. Waggler floats, on most occasions, are controlled by sinking the line to minimise the interference of the elements, whereas double rubber floats have to be controlled in a different way to prevent them skating about and dragging the bait around in an unnatural manner.

Sinking the line can be done in certain circumstances (see page 6), but the main requirement in keeping control over double rubber floats is to retain direct contact with them. The line between the rod tip and the float has to be kept as straight as possible. If it bows too much under the influence of current and/or wind the float will begin to skate across the current, and bites are deterred to the point where they cease altogether. You would look twice at your meal if the sausage jumped off the plate of its own volition, and fish are equally dubious when their feed behaves in unexpected ways!

Maintaining a reasonably straight line is fairly easy in calm conditions and anglers can cope with light winds from any direction if the flow is sufficient to help the straightening process. Strong winds, though, are a different matter. Upstream wind presents little problem, as does a wind coming upstream and away, or from behind. Even a down and out wind can be overcome, when the tackle is in experienced hands, but facers and howling downstreamers generally spell the end of double rubber fishing. When the line can be controlled, however, it is also possible to control the speed at which line is fed to the float. This, of course, gives anglers the capacity to put the float, and with it, the bait, through the swim at differing speeds. Many times a speed slower than the speed of the current proves right for catching, whereas full speed produces little or nothing.

The angler using wagglers has only the dragged shot method of slowing the tackle, give or take a few subtleties employed by the superstars which, I feel, might confuse matters if I discussed them here. The angler fishing double rubber rarely drags shot, but there are various things he can do to slow the speed. Some anglers allow the line to come off the reel and then through their fingers under light pressure. Others trap the line and release it a second or so later, thus causing the bait to swing up and down as it goes through the swim. The first method alters the presentation without doing much for the speed, but trapping the line at the reel and 'following' the float with the rod gives you absolute control of the speed for at least a short distance. Once the rod has followed as far as it can the line is released and the rod swept quickly back upstream. With experience it is possible to do this upstream sweep in such a way that the effect on the float is almost negligible, and then,

of course, the downstream 'follow' is repeated. When conditions permit the use of double rubber floats to maximum effect the results can be startling. Wagglers are effective, but no angler looks quite so good as a top-class angler going well with the double rubber. I have heard it likened to conducting an orchestra, and this is not far off the mark.

In addition to controlling the speed of the float, there is the original problem of keeping the line straight. In any conditions that are not perfect a bow will develop and will rapidly increase, so before it becomes large enough to interfere with the float it has to be dealt with or 'mended'. The line is trapped to prevent any more of it leaving the reel and the rod is lifted smoothly to straighten the bow. Then, as the float moves on downstream, the rod follows it from the high to low position. This retains control over the float speed in exactly the same way as the upstream to downstream follow. It has been necessary to cover these matters at some length, so that with this information you should have more chance of profiting from the following diagrams and text.

STICK FLOATS

Stick floats are one of the relatively few modern inventions which angling historians have not managed to trace back to Izaak Walton or even beyond. They have yet to celebrate their twentieth birthday, but they have become standard equipment for many all-round anglers. They are made from balsa wood and cane, the latter making a heavy base for the float and running for about two thirds of the length, and the balsa making a buoyant top third. They cast extremely well from the side position, and providing they are properly made they can present a bait beautifully in all manner of ways.

Some manufacturers make some quite good sticks these days, considering the difficulties of mass-production with materials of varying densities. (Balsa varies tremendously, and some cane is much heavier than others). Home production can pay, if you have the patience, but do watch what you buy. Some shops sell, as sticks, floats made entirely of hardwood, and whilst they will catch fish they will not perform all the tasks expected of the genuine stick float.

The floats were originally designed by Lancashire anglers for long casting, with lightly shotted tackle, across their canals, but it was soon discovered that they were the perfect tools for another job — catching roach 'on the drop' in rivers like the Trent. Evenly shotted with strings of No. 6 shot (Fig. 19), they presented an evenly falling bait to absolute perfection. They were fished in conjunction with a continuous stream of feed — mostly casters, in the early days — and the trick was to find the exact point and depth where the fish were intercepting the feed. With a well-timed check of the float the experts could

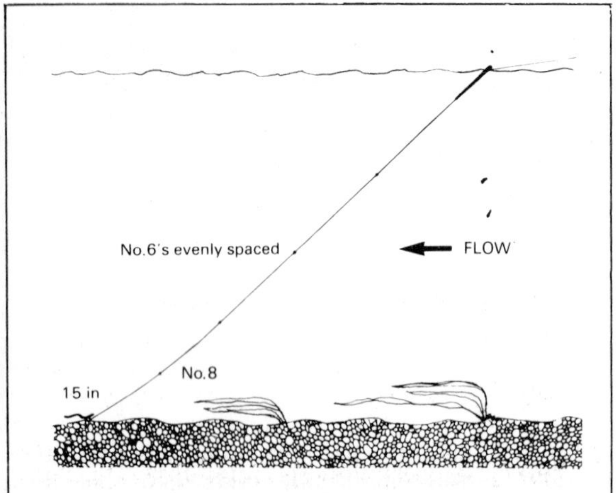

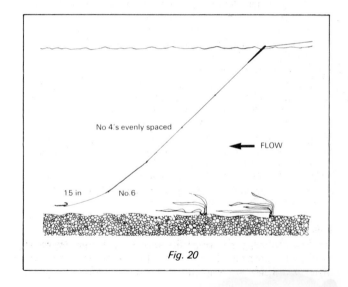

No.6's evenly spaced   ← FLOW

15 in   No.8

Fig. 19

No 4's evenly spaced   ← FLOW

15 in   No.6

Fig. 20

cause the hookbait to rise in the water and pop it straight into a fish's mouth! I have watched Kevin Ashurst catch a stone of Trent roach, and he was so in tune with his swim that he was able to tell me when every single bite was coming a second before it did! He put the bait in their mouthes with the precision of somebody feeding coins into a fruit machine. This anecdote is told to convince readers that float fishing is an art, as well as to acknowledge that much of my stick float knowledge emanates from the great Lancastrian. Sadly, the original string of No. 6s does not catch all that much on the drop these days, but it still catches plenty on or near the bottom when it is put through either even-paced or in a series of stop and start movements. As you may notice from the diagram, the float is being fished over-depth — an impossible ploy unless the float is controlled and very much slowed. The current working on the light shotting completes the trick.

A slightly bigger stick carrying a string of No. 4s, with a No. 6 near the hook instead of a No. 8, cannot be fished as far over-depth, except on some occasions when it is held back much harder. The rig shown in Fig. 20 will sometimes produce fish when the lighter No. 6 set-up will not, for reasons nobody has yet managed to explain to my satisfaction. In all probability, however, it is due to the mood of the fish on the day. It is because of their varying moods that it nearly always pays to change an approach which is not producing. Anglers should never stick with a losing method.

As always, the nature of the swim and the distance involved dictate how we should fish. Fishing a couple of feet of fastish water at close range can be achieved with a lightly shotted float fished well over-depth (Fig. 21), but the same swim at longer ranges would demand a bigger float carrying heavier shot (Fig.

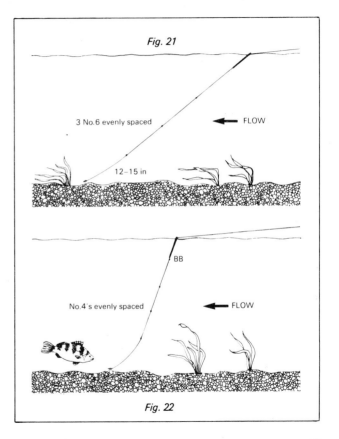

Fig. 21

3 No.6 evenly spaced

FLOW

12–15 in

BB

No.4's evenly spaced

FLOW

Fig. 22

22). This rig cannot be fished as much over-depth because of the heavier shot. In theory it should be possible to put most of the weight under the float and keep light shot on the line below, but it does not always work. Light shotting and long casting is a certain recipe for tackle tangles with sticks and many other floats. A light shot immediately below a heavy one is always prone to tangle. Whilst I have not specifically said so, every diagram in this book, which deals with strings of shot and varying sizes of shot, reflects the need to harmonise shot sizes in order to minimise tangle problems.

Since the early days anglers have found other uses for the stick not demanding strings of shot. The stick float is now commonly used for long casting into deeper water, where conditions permit, and Fig. 23 shows a typical set-up. The AAA shot tight under the float may seem a formidable amount of weight to add to the weight of the cane, but the BB at half depth (remember that a BB is half an AAA) is well-placed and sufficiently heavy to avoid casting tangles. Similarly the No. 4 (half a BB) shot is the right weight not to play bolas with the BB. Any tackle will tangle, though, if the cast is jerky or clumsy. A smooth sideways cast is always the requirement with the stick. The common overhead cast is a near guarantee of disaster. I would not advocate the use of the stick float in deepish fast water. Other floats can handle the job better, but for those who fancy the big stick, Fig. 24 shows a suitable set-up.

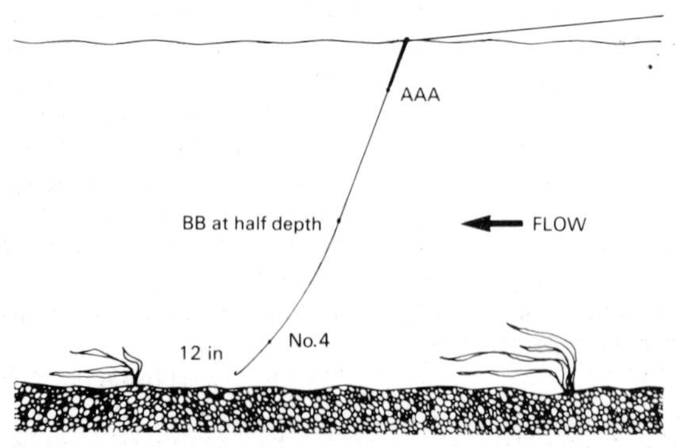

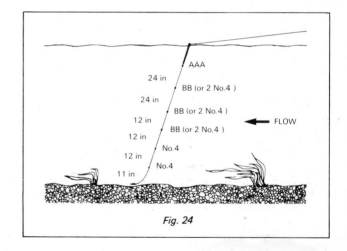

Fig. 23

Fig. 24

There is one unusual stick float rig worth illustrating for those who are determined to make a stick work in adverse conditions, see Fig. 25 which shows a routine stick float rig with the line sunk, with the aid of a No. 6 shot pinched on the line above the float. There are times when this approach will catch fish when the more obvious choice of a waggler float will not, but it is not a big weight method. It is a struggle method more applicable for match fishing; fun fishers would probably opt for an easier life, for there is no doubt that it is difficult to fish double rubber with the line sunk.

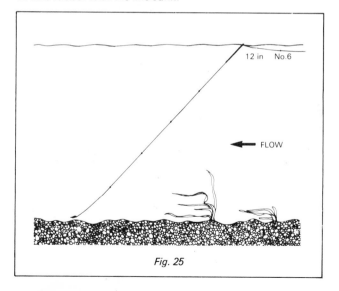

12 in   No.6

← FLOW

Fig. 25

WIRE-STEMMED STICKS AND AVONS

When notable anglers like Billy Lane decry the stick float and advance the rival claims of the wire-stemmed stick and the Avon, sensible anglers should listen. But I have listened, and I do not think that the great man is altogether right on this one. I certainly agree with him that there is a place for a wire-stemmed stick, which has the same balsa body as the standard stick, with a length of piano wire instead of the cane stem. But I have found that, size for size, the wire-stemmed stick can do most of the jobs that an ordinary stick can handle. It is not quite so good at presenting a slow falling bait, but it does have more stability. It 'grips' the water much better than a stick float and this enables the angler to mend his line more easily without dragging the float off course. That being the case, the wire-stemmed stick is perhaps a better proposition for the beginner than the standard stick. But something has to be lost for the float to gain the extra grip, and for my money what is lost is the delicacy of the stick; it does not respond so readily to the will of the angler. Most of the stick float shottings can be used with the wire-stemmed stick.

As for the Avon, I think that Billy Lane used to be right, but not any more. His original affection for the Avon developed in the days before the stick, when Avons were made from large crowquills with cork for the bodies. These were, indeed, superb floats, and made in the old way they are still everything that

Billy Lane claims for them. Unfortunately, the supply of suitable bird feathers could never be adequate, and neither quill nor cork lent themselves to mass-production methods.

The only relation modern Avons have with the old ones is the approximate shape. The stems and tips are now hard cane, and the bodies are made of balsa. The tips of these floats are virtually nil in the buoyancy department, whereas the old crowquill tip fought to stay up top. Modern Avon floats go under as soon as the hook touches bottom and, whilst I would bow to Billy Lane as a float angler, I just cannot make them work. I take it as some sort of tacit support that I have never seen a modern Avon used in a club match, a big open, a National Championship, superstar invitation event or the World Championship. Thousands, maybe even millions, are made each year, and I often wonder what happens to them.

BALSA FLOATS

The deeper and heavier flowing the swim, the more lead shot is needed on the line. It is used to counteract the effects of the flow and to present a nice steady bait to fish on the bottom. Stick floats cannot cope because they do not carry sufficient weight. Wagglers carry the weight, but heavy flowing swims sweep bottom-only floats away too quickly. What is required is a material capable of supporting lots of weight and which, at the same time, is not too bulky. Balsa floats certainly look bulky, when compared with their slim cousins, the sticks, but they can work to deadly effect.

The floats are easily made from round balsa wood, which is obtainable from handicraft or model shops, and are readily available from all good tackle shops. Sizes can range from a couple of BB right up to 3½ swan, though I do not think there are all that many uses for the smaller ones. My interest starts at 3AAA, and I have two more in between that and the 3½ swan.

The trick with balsas is to get the bait down fast to where the fish are, and make sure it stays there. These requirements dictate the shotting; it is all on the last 4 ft of line, there is nothing very sophisticated about it. The shotting for the 3AAA float can be seen in Fig. 26. Two of the AAAs are set 4 ft from

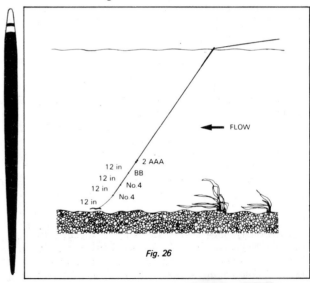

Fig. 26

the hook, the other AAA is split into a BB and a couple of No. 4s, evenly spaced at intervals of 12 in. This and all the other balsas are fished held back hard; with all that weight below and the strong flow helping to keep everything straight, I would say that there is not an easier float to control. A ploy which often works is to hold back so hard that the float is held still for a few seconds. Until the current gets to work, this momentarily stops the bait, too, and it often produces a bite.

As they are hard held, the balsas are invariably fished over-depth; if they were not the flow would lift the bait over the fishes' heads. The need to keep it down demands the use of a fairly heavy terminal shot. I rarely use a bottom shot as big as a No. 4 with other floats, unless I am dragging one to slow a big waggler down. But a No. 4 is the smallest terminal shot to contemplate when using a balsa float. I do not think twice about using a BB or even an AAA, and I have even seen top anglers using 3½ swan shot all bunched together about 2 ft from the hook. Admittedly they were fishing that way to hold down very big, buoyant baits in quick water. Try shotting up a great lump of wasp grub cake, it takes at least a swan shot to hold it down; crusts and bread flake require an AAA. So, whilst Fig. 26 shows the routine shotting for the biggest of the balsa floats, remember that it can be varied.

SLIDER FLOATS

Up to now I have been careful to avoid the problem which arises when the angler has to fish water that is deeper than the rod is long. Highly experienced anglers can fish 15 ft with a 12 ft rod and some actually profess to prefer struggling in this manner. For some reason they do not get on with the sliding float, though I cannot understand why. I think there is a case for using a slider on water over 10 ft deep. Fixed floats set at 10 ft on a 12 ft rod are forever twiddling round the rod tip as the angler rebaits or unhooks a fish, especially on windy days.

There is no real mystery about the sliders. They are merely floats which will cope with depths which fixed floats cannot easily cope with, and because they cope with greater depths they have to be on the large side. The balsa slider, for example,

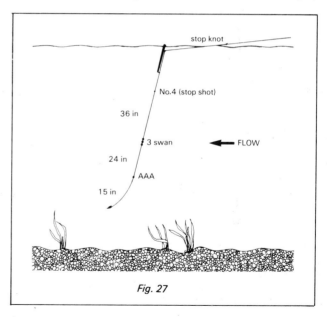

Fig. 27

is usually 3½ to 4 swan. It differs in shape only slightly from the floats in the balsa range. Instead of being attached double rubber it has a large wire ring at the base, which is slightly offset. Whipped just under the tip of the float is another ring. It is lined up with the bottom ring but its diameter is much smaller; it is sufficiently small to stop sliding when it comes up against the stop knot tied on the reel line, as shown in Fig. 3. This knot, when properly tied, can be moved about under strong finger pressure, so enabling the angler to adjust the setting in his search for exactly the right depth. Once it has been set correctly, the float can be fished in much the same way as the biggest of the double rubber balsa floats.

The shotting differs very little, as Fig. 27 shows. The only real difference is that the No. 4 shot is set 6 ft or 7 ft from the hook; this is solely to stop the float sliding too far down the line.

These big floats demand the use of heavy line — at least 3 lb — to prevent breaks on the strike; this advice applies to all the big floats, whatever family they belong to. Casting with balsa sliders is child's play. With all that weight working for you an underhand swing takes them a long way, but they are not quite as versatile as the double rubber equivalent. Hard checked, the slider tends to lift up a lot. It has to be run through at or very near the speed of the current or allowed to run through with the bottom shot dragging to slow it down.

For close-range work in deep flowing water a large goose quill makes an effective slider, as does another double ring slider, which is still seen occasionally — the porcupine quill (the large variety). However, balsa sliders have virtually relegated both of them to the museum, though bird quills will never die out altogether. To this day they are better than some floats we commonly see on sale.

Double ring sliders are generally seen less often than bottom ring sliders which are, of course, sliding wagglers. These are mostly used on deep stillwaters and the big, slow rivers and

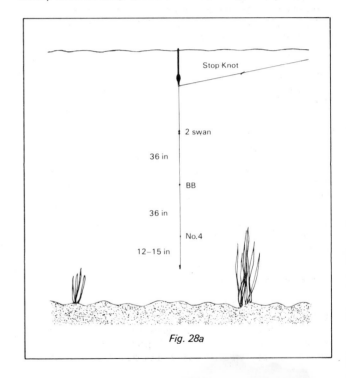

Fig. 28a

drains like those found in the Fenlands. The size range is from 1 swan up to 3 swan; the small ones are used mostly for still or very slow water at fairly close-range and the bigger ones for more distant and deeper water. The diagrams, Figs. 28a and 28b show how the lighter and heavier floats are shotted, but the only real difference is the weights. The pattern is nearly always the same — bulk shot about 7 ft from the hook, small shot about 12 in to 15 in from the hook and another shot, usually twice the size of the terminal shot, half-way between that and the bulk.

Reading the behaviour of sliding floats is an interesting and often rewarding pastime. Immediately after the cast they lie flat on the surface as the shots pull through the bottom ring which, of course, has a very small diameter — just large enough to allow free passage of the line. When the bulk shot gets right down and the stop knot hits the ring, the float sits up. The next thing to watch for is the further lowering of the float as the middle shot registers, and after that the terminal shot sinks the float down to the required 'show' above the surface. Each of these separate movements must be watched and mentally timed. If you notice that something has not happened when it should have, it is very likely a bite. Hold-up bites often come when you are slider fishing, usually because fish start coming off the bottom to intercept feed. Frequent hold-up bites suggest a gradual shortening of the depth being fished; bites often become more frequent still if the hookbait is presented accurately at the feeding level. I always think of hold-up bites in terms of a person snatching a sandwich off a passing tray. He would probably eat more heartily if the food was sitting in front of him on a table!

Before leaving the subject of sliders it is necessary to mention the fact that the depth of the water is not the only factor influencing their use. I have already mentioned that they can make life a little easier when fishing swims only 10 ft deep, but sometimes the nature of the surroundings demand the use of a slider. If you are fishing with a high bank behind you or among dense undergrowth, you can encounter difficulties in casting a fairly modest length of line. Underhand swings with slider tackle can overcome the problem.

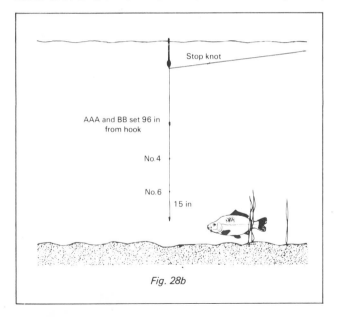

Stop knot

AAA and BB set 96 in from hook

No. 4

No. 6

15 in

Fig. 28b

LOADED FLOATS

There are some who say there is no need for loaded floats; that the conventional floats will do the same jobs. I have never been sure which side of the fence to stand on this one. The fact that I hardly ever use them is not much of a guide to my true feelings, because loaded floats are specialised weapons designed for particular purposes. 'Loaded' means that most of the weight required to cock them is built into the base of the float during manufacture. They are so designed to fish at long range in shallow water, and at the same time eliminating the need to put much shot on the line.

The most well known, I suppose, of the loaded floats is the zoomer designed by Leicester anglers to fish the far side of the River Welland — a considerable cast. Their floats had so much brass stuffed up the bottom that they were probably quite lethal, had anyone got in the way. Because of all the weight the float had to be given a dumpy body to prevent it spearing deep down into the water. The stem was made from slim cane, a material which is much more sensitive than the peacock quill of the normal waggler. It is the perfect material for signalling lift and drop bites at long range, which was the main object of the exercise. The zoomer is a classic example of how the circumstances and the aims influence the design of floats. The typical shotting pattern is shown in Fig. 29 but be warned, the zoomer is not a float for beginners. The main problem that the newcomer will encounter is tangling on the cast, a fate which befell me about once every three casts when I first tried to master this float.

There are many other loaded floats — usually with brass welding rod in the base — but the majority are of little relevance here. Most of them have 'duplicates' in the non-loaded field,

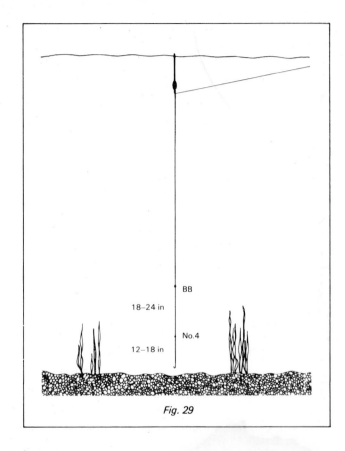

Fig. 29

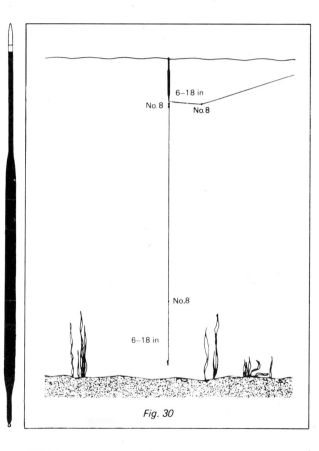

Fig. 30

though two which are still relevant, perhaps, are Billy Lane's Dart and the Drinking Straw. The dart is a balsa-bodied, thin cane-tipped float with brass insert (a longer casting version of the Canal Antenna) and the loading leaves the float carrying no more than a few dust shots. It is an extremely sensitive float designed for fishing across canals. To all intents and purposes it is a miniature zoomer, though it lacks a body. It is fished, like all bottom-only floats, with the line sunk; although being relatively light it usually requires a shot above the float to help the line under (see Fig. 30). It signals bites on the drop very well, and it can be pulled under without the fish feeling much in the way of resistance. It has the zoomer's capacity to tangle on the cast in inexperienced hands.

The drinking straw is an interesting float. There was a time when top Sheffield anglers were making this float work for roach on the River Witham, and more recently it has been used by Southern anglers for far bank fishing for chub in shallow water. They liked it because it fell very lightly, without scaring the fish — mainly the wary chub. I am not sure whether the Southern anglers fished with the straw loaded, but the Sheffield anglers certainly did. They put brass rod up the bottom end of the straw (plastic variety) and sealed the other end by melting it with a match. They found it extremely sensitive for the Witham's shy biting roach, and they were hitting bites which they had missed with other floats.

Nowadays the pole has provided them with an even more efficient means of hitting those fish, and the straw has sunk into limbo. But it is worth mentioning because it is cheap and an easy float to make. Young anglers should certainly consider it for fishing on ponds — for which work it should be shotted like a light waggler (see Fig. 10) They can be made loaded or unloaded, the latter design requiring a cane plug in the base with a ring whipped to it, instead of the brass. If you have difficulty in heat-sealing the tips, just plug them with some balsa wood instead.

The most practical use of loaded floats that I have encountered was demonstrated to me once by Stuart Thompson, a Leeds angler, who was having a tremendous run at the time with the waggler float in matches on the River Witham. Stuart had loaded all his wagglers by winding lead wire on the base, between the body and the eye. The object was to make each float, regardless of size, take exactly the same amount of shot on the line. That way he always knew where he was with his shotting, and if conditions changed and demanded a heavier or a smaller float he could change without having to touch his shotting. Being a canny Yorkshireman, Stuart did not fix the required amount of lead wire permanently in position. For different uses, on other rivers, he could remove the wire and fish with more lead on the line.

MISCELLANEOUS FLOATS

Since I became one of the founders and editors of *Coarse Angler* magazine one question has continually arisen in letters from young anglers. How to strike successfully at the bites? Young anglers do so many things wrong that it is difficult to advise them with any confidence that their particular problem will be solved. Attention to some of the basics covered in this book can work wonders for many of them, but there are times when the fish are clever enough to tax the minds of highly experienced anglers.

I can remember two waters where missed bites baffled me — one a big and hard-fished city reservoir and the other a small but equally hard-fished club pond. In both places the fish invariably rose off the bottom to intercept loose feed, but, because they knew all about anglers and their baits, catching them was a nightmare. They would bite like greased lightning and eject the bait at the merest hint of resistance.

The reservoir problem was solved by changing the feeding method. Groundbaiting with breadcrumb was banned, but a soil and sand mixture packed solid with maggots and casters kept the fish on the bottom. Fishing a bait hard on the bottom produced much slower bites that were more easily hit.

The small pond problem was not solved until I invented a special float. The targets were perch, which would hurl themselves at loose feed, but, whatever conventional float was fished, they would eject the bait in a flash if it had a hook in it. It was possible to catch some, but the number of missed bites was amazing. Groundbaiting was banned on the pond, too, so I set about developing a method which would cut out resistance for a couple of seconds after a fish had taken the bait. After several attempts I produced a float and a rig which did the trick and I call it the Surface Slider (Fig. 31). I made it from one-third of a drinking straw. Each end was plugged with balsa and also at each end I glued in a tiny offset ring.

The float was fixed by the line passing through the rings and the knot attaching the hook length to the reel line prevented it from sliding down to the hook. At the top side of the float, 2 ft away, I tied a sliding stop knot. The float was therefore free on the line between the two knots. I almost invariably fished it unshotted because the fish came near the surface and, eventually, boiled under the loose feed. A fish could take a bait

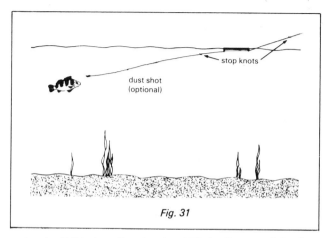

dust shot
(optional)

stop knots

Fig. 31

and swim 2 ft before the stop knot hit the float, and the float itself offered next to no resistance.

Bite detection was a piece of cake! The line just slid through the rings and the slight friction caused the float to tow across the surface. If the strike was delayed until the stop knot hit, the float speeded up tremendously, but I rarely left it that long. The results were remarkable; I caught 10 lb of little perch in a two-hour evening match, a weight never approached before or since. Having solved the problem, I abandoned this method as the interest had gone. I do not expect the surface slider to sweep the country, but I can see other applications for it. I would think that those anglers who dedicate a large part of their angling lives to the catching of huge bleak weights in matches might find it useful.

A group of Barnsley anglers have perfected a method of watching fish take the maggot bait and they are thinking in terms of producing bleak catches of 35 lb plus in five-hour matches. One of them, Tom Pickering, has already done this in practice. Watching the maggot is their way of solving the resistance problem. When it disappears they assume that it is in a fish's mouth and strike. The floats that they use for this big weight method are short lengths of flat porcupine quill, attached double rubber. It is possible that the slider ring attachment could give them a secondary method of defeating resistance, which might marginally improve their catches. They will not know, of course, until they try it, but trying something new is one of the things which makes float fishing such an interesting pastime.

Every single float that I have described so far is the result of somebody, in the recent or long distant past, identifying a problem and finding out how to deal with it. Once anglers understand that, they are on the road to fishing correctly, with the right float, nearly every time. And this produces the catches which seldom seemed to come before!

My surface slider is not unlike the flat peacock quill method once described by Kevin Ashurst and I know it works bewilderingly well at times. Fig. 32 practically tells all; a small piece of peacock is fastened double rubber and it is fished on or just off the bottom with a couple of little shot. The bites, when they come, are fantastic. The float tears away across the surface, turns upside down and crash dives like a stricken submarine. Quite why it works in such a spectacular fashion is something neither Kevin nor I can explain. It is basically a stillwater method, but a float/leger variation (Fig. 33) also works well at times on slow rivers, when the fish are demanding a dead still bait.

One truly classic example of an angler thinking cleverly to solve a problem is the wasp grub float developed by well-known Yorkshire angler, Alec Lambourne. He and a group of his friends made names for themselves by discovering that winter chub would accept wasp grub baits preserved in a deep freeze.

Previously this had been a highly seasonal, though deadly, bait for chub. Mostly they legered the wasp grub cake on the far side of deep, wide rivers like the Yorkshire Ouse, but Alec noticed that sometimes the chub would take the cake off the top. Wasp cake is so buoyant that it comes off and rises to the

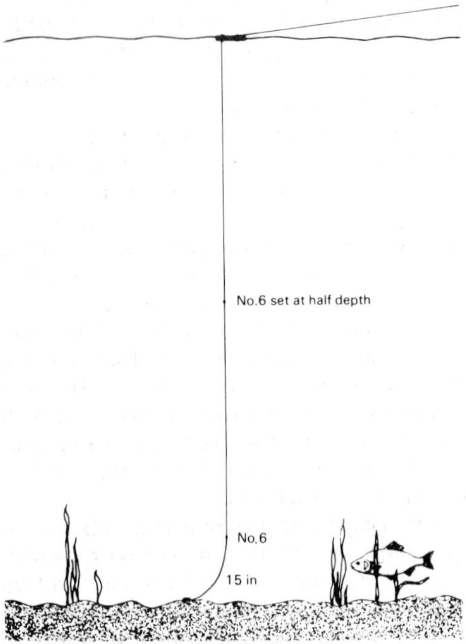

No.6 set at half depth

No.6

15 in

Fig. 32

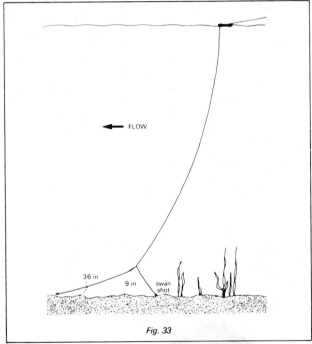

FLOW

36 in

9 in

swan shot

Fig. 33

surface as soon as a leger angler starts to reel in, and the sight of chub slashing at it like trout after flies was too much for Alec. He needed a float which would cast grub cake huge distances and the ingenious result is illustrated here (see Fig. 34). The body is made from round, half-inch balsa. The round top is cork and it is attached to the body via a meat skewer, the eye of which forms a ring at the top. In the base of the float, believe it or not, is a 4 in nail with sufficient lead wrapped around it to sink the float so that only the round top remains above the surface. It may sound crude, but when I saw Alec making it work I could scarcely believe it. He struck off a few pieces of legered cake and the chub boiled at them. He hurled a piece across with a powerful 14 ft rod, and he was into a chub in seconds. He watched for the boil, but struck only when the diving chub had taken the float down. Attaching the float is a simple job; the line is passed through the top eye and the float is trapped in place with a split shot on either side. Alec recommends leaving about 4 ft of line from float to hook.

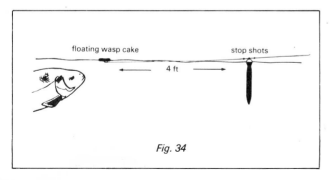

floating wasp cake

stop shots

4 ft

Fig. 34

FLOATS FOR PREDATORS

A great angling writer once offered the thought that floats were pleasing in their appearance and even more pleasing in their disappearance. When I first read this I began to wonder which float's disappearance pleased and excited me the most. The answer had to be a float supporting a live or deadbait in water known to hold monster pike. The fish responsible might be a tiddler, but until it is struck and played it could also be the page one lead in the angling papers!

Pike fishing used to be the crude end of the angling game, as far as tackle was concerned. Now, thanks to thoughtful and inventive anglers, terminal tackles and floats are much more satisfactory. Little is seen, these days, of the old *Fishing Gazette* 'bung' which was standard equipment for livebaiting when I first pointed a boat into that one-time wonderland, the Upper Thurne area of the Norfolk Broads. The bung was a spherical object of almost cricket ball proportions, with a central hole and a slot for the line. It was jammed on the line in the required place with a large wooden peg and it was difficult to imagine anything capable of offering greater resistance to a taking pike. The bung survives to this day, slightly miniaturised, but I will try to make this just about the first beginners' book not to illustrate the monstrosity.

Suitable alternatives are now readily available, in streamlined cigar shapes with central holes. They come in a variety of sizes for use with all types and sizes of live and dead baits, from gudgeon to large roach, or even mackerel. The basic method of fishing with them has changed little over the years. The float is fixed on the line via the central hole, and the most common means of setting the depth is with a small silicon rubber float ring, through which the line is passed twice. This easily adjusts when required, and on pike rods, which have fairly large diameter rings, this form of stop will usually pass through them on the cast. When I am fishing water much deeper than the length of the rod, however, I prefer to use the sliding stop knot (Fig. 3 on page 6). This also demands the use of a small bead above the float, to prevent the stop knot going through the hole in the float. It is a very efficient and effective method. I tie the stop knot with 6/8lb line on reel lines of around 12lbs breaking strain. The diagrams, Figs. 35 and 36, show how the floats are fished. In shallow water up to 4ft I prefer a bait to swim free without any lead on the line.

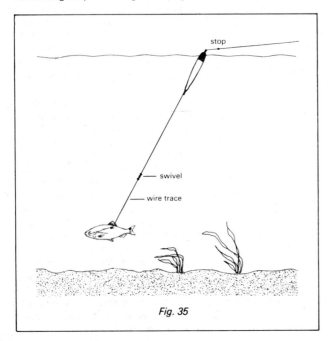

Fig. 35

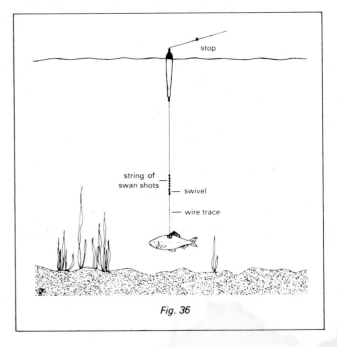

Fig. 36

It can swim anywhere from bottom to surface, but in deeper water I encourage the bait to stay down with the use of a barrel lead or a string of swan shots on the line immediately above the trace — the wire to which the hooks are attached. These are used to prevent the pike biting free, for its teeth are

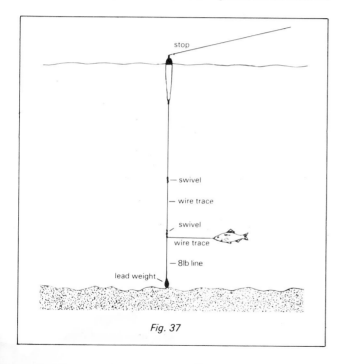

stop

— swivel

— wire trace

swivel

wire trace

— 8lb line

lead weight

Fig. 37

very sharp, and can easily sever the strongest monofilament line. Traces can be bought in tackle shops, but once the beginner knows what is required he can easily make his own. A prime object in livebaiting is to match the float to the size of the bait, using the smallest float possible. This allows the bait to cover a fairly large area without tiring it unduly, though there are times when it is necessary or desirable to anchor a bait in one place. For this job a paternoster rig is required (see Fig. 37). Since I learned my pike fishing on the Norfolk Broads, where the free swimming livebait was the best method, I was a bit slow to appreciate the value of paternosters, and have changed my mind a lot since this book was first written.

Paternosters are ideal for anchoring baits in confined spaces, near weedbeds or in between overhanging trees and bushes. They also hold a bait by the far shelf on fenland drain fisheries, and they allow you to keep the bait where you want it on flowing waters. In addition, a paternostered bait keeps livlier for longer, and some days it proves easily the deadliest method. At other times, usually in the colder conditions, a dead fish is more effective — either a natural inhabitant of fresh water or the smellier sea fish such as herring, mackerel, sprat or smelt. The smell of these baits is a key factor, and could be the reason why they sometimes work even better if they are cut in half.

There is considerable argument these days over the moral aspects of livebaiting, but this is better left to the individual angler. There is too much interference, often from anglers and angling officials with no direct interest in pike fishing. It has resulted in rules and byelaws which inhibit the sport quite considerably — so much so that rules are now quite openly flouted. Laws which people do not want to obey, and cannot be made to stick, are bad laws, and we have too many already. There is nothing to prevent the individual angler deciding his own limits, and limiting himself to dead baits if he wishes, but he will catch many fewer pike than I will in the same number of rod hours.

There is little point in illustrating the suspended deadbait method, for on paper it looks almost exactly the same as the livebait tackle. The main difference is that less lead is required; in fact in most cases none is required. Dead fish sink well enough if the swim bladder is punctured and all the air is squeezed out. Apart from suspending them in one place, it can also work to cast them across the wind and allow the wind to blow them round in a wide semi-circle. Especially when little or no lead is used the bait will swing round in a gently, undulating manner which gives it some semblance of life. It must look like a stricken, dying fish to a pike — just the sort of easy meal a hungry predator prefers. Curiously it is not, in my experience, a method which catches a lot of pike, but when they come they tend to be big ones. It used to be my proud boast that I had never caught a pike under 12 lb on a large, drifted deadbait, but eventually I came unstuck!

Legering deadbaits — casting them out without using floats — is held to be the most efficient way of catching pike with dead fish. The theory cannot be faulted, but it is open to misuse. It is easy for an inattentive angler to miss seeing his line peeling out until the pike responsible has swallowed the bait and a set of deadly treble hooks. The problem is multiplied when several rods are in use at the same time, which seems to be fashionable these days. Using floats in conjunction with a deadbait presented on the bottom may not be quite so efficient, but the float is a better bite warning system. Somehow one 'sees' it go even when not exactly watching it; at times I have actually heard it go.

In some parts of the country, mainly in fisheries radiating from the Relief Channel at King's Lynn, anglers can now fish for another exciting predator — the zander. Having never fished for zander, I know nothing about them first hand. But

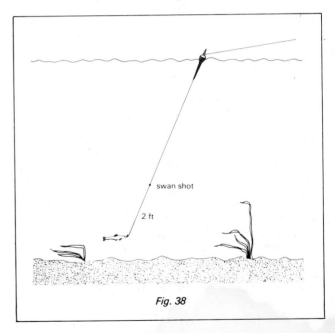

swan shot

2 ft

Fig. 38

it seems obvious from the writings of those who do that small live and deadbaits are the order of the day and that they are fished on scaled-down pike tackles.

After the pike, my personal favourite predator is the pugnacious perch. Having been fortunate enough to catch them to 3 lb 7 oz, with many of them weighing over 2 lb, I am in a position to join the argument about their fighting qualities. I know of no 2 lb coarse fish which can outfight a 2 lb perch and I have caught 2 lb examples of every coarse fish capable of growing to and beyond that weight except zander and grayling.

Beyond question the best way to catch big perch is with a livebait or a lobworm. The latter can be offered with whichever of the earlier floats is appropriate for the circumstances or with the leger. The livebait, using gudgeon, minnow or small dace for preference, is best fished on the perch bob float. This float is a monstrosity for any other purpose, but for some reason it is the most misused of the entire range. In any group of six youngsters fishing for tiddlers around a park pond, two or three will be using a perch bob. The blame for it rests solely upon the shoulders of the tackle trade or that section of it which cares only for profit. The one way to fish a perch bob to maximum effect is with a livebait as shown in Fig. 38. The bait is presented just clear of the bottom and is free to swim anywhere in the bottom four feet if a single swan shot is placed two feet from the hook. This rig is nearly always used for perch on stillwater, but it works on rivers for perch, chub and trout. Small livebaits also catch pike and if pike are the primary target the hook has to be attached to a wire trace.

Float-making Materials

During the course of this book I have mentioned many of the basic materials from which floats can be made. For those who may have been stimulated to the point where they think they would like to try making their own I should, perhaps, cover some of the materials I have not already mentioned. Had I gone through the whole range in the general text it would have been confusing. I shall not even attempt that here, for many materials in common use are usually mere substitutes for something better.

I was the first to publicise sarkandas reed, mainly because it surfaced at a time when peacock quill was almost impossible to obtain. It is an easier material than peacock to work with (though more difficult to paint), but it is not quite as buoyant. Sarkandas floats, therefore, end up bigger than peacocks for a given shot-carrying capacity and this is not always a good thing. On the other hand, the lower buoyancy means that floats which are more sensitive than peacock quill can be made. This is a tricky area for discussion, as it usually brings me into conflict with Archimedes' principle. So, I shall try to avoid looking like the failure in the sciences which I undoubtedly was and content myself with saying that in my practical experience — and that of others — sarkandas floats often register bites that are better and more easy to hit than the equivalent float in peacock. Why it is I do not know, but it is true. I can recall that fine Bradford angler, John Illingworth, telling me that a mere pimple of crowquill disappearing would produce bites that were easier to hit than the same pimple of peacock. Since he was busily proving it before my very eyes and the same switch worked for me, I believed it. The switch has since worked for me many times, yet it defies logical explanation and an 'O' level scientist can probably prove that I am talking nonsense! So, there is still a case for using sarkandas, even though peacock quill is now more easily available.

The reed should be viewed as an addition, not a substitute for peacock. I find the former particularly effective when fish are biting infrequently and shyly, especially in winter at close range, and on slow and stillwater. I make several floats from it, though these days I generally use the reed as a tip insert in peacock quill. It keeps the overall size down for a given shot-carrying capacity, which gives a marginal improvement in casting qualities, and also offers less resistance on the strike.

Another material worth mentioning in the same context is close-grained polystyrene. It is pale blue in colour — sometimes white — and whilst it can be bought, it can also be found lying around building sites. It is used for insulating and packaging purposes, but much of it is wasted. Scrap pieces can make excellent pike floats and waggler float bodies can be fashioned with the aid of an electric drill and some patience. A way though has to be found to jam a block of polystyrene in place in the chuck for long enough to shape the body with sandpaper or whatever. Former England International, Terry Payne, who taught me how to do the job, uses a lathe with the polystyrene on a square mandrel — the polystyrene soon begins to turn on a round one and so brings the shaping to an abrupt halt! The original hole in the polystyrene is achieved with a quick thrust from a hot needle; if it is done too slowly the resulting hole is too big.

Heavy cane is usually used for the base of stick floats, but I am assured that fibreglass is equally as good. Glass and balsa sticks are available in some shops. Light cane can be used in

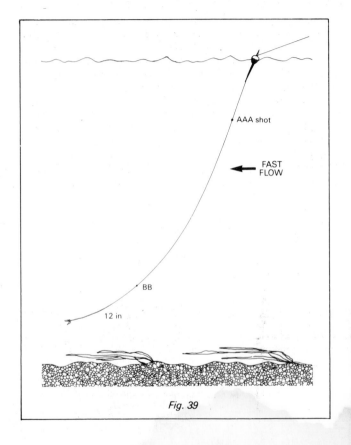

AAA shot

FAST FLOW

BB

12 in

Fig. 39

much the same way as sarkandas for tip inserts in waggler floats. It is so sensitive, though, that it is effective mostly in stillwaters at close range. If conditions are perfect, it can be used at longer range or on very slow water if the hookbait is presented off the bottom. If the bait does drag bottom, the cane is not sufficiently buoyant to hold it up.

I have already referred to the porcupine quill as a slider and a flat bleak float, but whole porcupine quills, fished double rubber were relied upon by many anglers as nice, stable trotting floats before the advent of the stick float. Some anglers still use them to this day. Certainly a short quill fitted with a blob of balsa just below the tip is an admirable float for grayling fishing in fast, rough water (see Fig. 39) — this is something I have learnt since I started writing this book. This is the fascination of float fishing. Learning the basics is a relatively simple proposition. Knowing it all is impossible !

The author with his catch of two fine pike.

35

Index